Don Benson Books

About the author

Don Benson was born and raised in the North East of England. He has had an interest in historical works from childhood, first experiencing the genre through the Horrible Histories series. From here his interest grew and he read every book he could get his hands on, devouring the knowledge within the pages. Now, Don has begun writing his own books seeking to aid others in discovering a love of history. In his professional life he has worked in and alongside a number of museums and historical associations, re-enactment groups and primary schools. From these he has a wealth of experience and knowledge which he draws on when creating his books.

Chapter Guide

1. Chapter Guide
2. Introduction
3. Curriculum
4. Introducing the Topic
5. The First Step
6. Drama
7. Food
8. Educational Visits
9. Subject Knowledge
10. Local Area
11. Rewards and Extra Curricular Activities
12. Display
13. Partnerships
14. Music
15. Famous People

16. Experimental Archaeology
17. ICT
18. DT
19. Art
20. PE
21. History in EYFS
22. Home Learning/Busy Tray Activities
23. How History Links to Modern Issues
24. Conclusions
25. Acknowledgement

Introduction

History is a subject which has often been shunned as boring. The common thought is that it is a trawl through dusty old textbooks on the deaths of kings from five hundred years ago. It is no mistake that the National Curriculum does not aim to encourage fostering a love of history amongst children but focuses rather on their understanding of concepts such as empire or peasantry and using their own own knowledge in different historical contexts. Although these are admirable targets, true understanding of a subject is only achieved when it appeals to more than the forced learning of its contents in order to reach government standards. A passionate student is a student that has already half conquered the hardest part of learning. Despite the mention of curiosity it offers little help in this regard, almost mentioning it as a passing thought, 'just in case it appeals', sort of target. History is only boring if it is made boring. I cannot stress this enough.

I have always been interested in history and have spent years watching documentaries, reading books, visiting and taking part in re-enactments and collecting items of historical interest and yet at school I found my history lessons dull, disengaging and disinteresting. For me this was no big problem, my interest in history was founded by my family and was constantly re-affirmed but for others in my class all it did was present the subject in a boring, flat manner. Every lesson was spent the same way, a slideshow was shown on the board or a worksheet was projected, whilst the teacher talked us through it, then we were given the worksheet and told to answer the questions.

Occasionally we would be asked to cut and stick in order to create a timeline. Only two lessons in my entire time in primary school have retained any significance. The first is when our teacher led us in a project to create our own air raid shelter where we made the entire garden (a shoe box), the shelter (from corrugated card), and the interior (dolls house furniture or made with bits and pieces like bottle caps) to create what amounted to an excellent and well remembered lesson. The other was a video of a granddad taking his grandchildren on a time travel adventure, the only one from the series we saw. At the time it was new and exciting and engaged us all and for a week the effort seemed to improve, even playground conversations turned to it. But all too soon we had returned to the old way.

In this book drawing from my own experiences of studying history, and working in a primary school as both an on the ground practitioner and a member of the strategic team, I will discuss methods and actions to make history fun and engaging for all children and hopefully staff too. The suggestions and methods in this book should not be adhered to as a strict guide or used to replace a curriculum but used more as an inspiration for similar or adapted activities in order to support the schools interpretation of the curriculum. It is worth noting that although there will be references to the National Curriculum at the time of writing these may change and it is the responsibility of the reader to check these are still relevant.

From my own experience I know that practitioners are expected to be counsellors, office workers, judges, jurors, police officers, health and safety experts, nurses, curriculum developers, politicians, cleaners, all knowing beings and computer technicians on top of being educators. Hopefully this book will help you be a historian and offer a quick path to boost your planning and make finding resources easy. Teachers and school staff should be praised constantly for the hard work they do. I hope this book helps lessen the load. Remember your wellbeing is more important than anything else in this book.

The history of Britain and the world as a whole is a fascinating interconnected web of strange goings on and insane coincidences such as the events leading up to the First World War. Why then do so many people hate it?

Typically the answers are the same. Memorise these dates, these names and these famous people. If you can list every King and Queen of England since Aethelred the Unready that is a worthy achievement but it does not mean you are equipped to teach history in an engaging way. Understanding that history also encapsulates the lives of the ordinary folk and knowing that history doesn't change, only our interpretation of what happened is a primary objective of a historian.

Often people get caught up in incorrect history and are unable to fully grasp that our understanding of history has changed and more evidence has emerged. For example how often have you heard people assert that the German army during the Second World War had the best tanks in the form of the Tiger variant? (Your answer may be never which means that either, you have surrounded yourself with knowledgeable historians or that you have no interest in the intricacies of WW2 armoured warfare. If the latter is the case I salute you as someone who made a better decision than I did.) A tank which was too heavy to cross difficult ground effectively, that was too slow and too large to disguise from air attack convincingly, that had a poor fuel system and was difficult to maintain and repair in the field. After the war the Allies did not adopt the Tiger design but rather improved their own designs, speaking to their effectiveness.

History as a topic is only boring if you allow it to be boring, a point I cannot stress enough (again). For yourself, find the piece of history you enjoy and delve deep. For your students, help them find their favourite part of history and explore it in their own way. Hopefully, what you read in this book will work to inspire you, to expand your resources and give you access to websites that will improve your teaching of history. No matter how experienced a teacher you are there will always be some improvement to be found. With so much time spent jumping through hoops, filling out paperwork and trying to plan lessons this book aims to lessen the workload in the area of history.

The aim of this book is in essence to be used in concert with, and support of the school wide history plan. There are many different resource sites, tried and tested ideas and example plans that will be useful for planning, preparing resources and creating an enjoyable historical environment. All research and resources for this book have been gathered from or tested in British primary schools that have been rated as Outstanding or Good with outstanding elements by OFSTED.

Each activity in this book has been tried on a number of occasions and has been successfully adapted for equality and diversity, differentiation, class size, and age group. Use this book as a tool to find and create engaging history topics rather than seeing it as a checklist of things that must be done. Everything in this book is a framework of suggestions and creativity to enable staff access to plans and resources that they may not have time to find in their usual busy lives. A great many of these activities have also been implemented by youth groups, childcare groups and parents, though these have usually been adapted. Remember that the most powerful thing you can use to teach history is yourself. Without your constant efforts to become a better educator and your personal hard work and success, this book would be useless as would all of the resources, links and plans within.

Curriculum

A high-quality history education will help pupils gain a coherent knowledge and understanding of Britain's past and that of the wider world. It should inspire pupils' curiosity to know more about the past. Teaching should equip pupils to ask perceptive questions, think critically, weigh evidence, sift arguments, and develop perspective and judgement. History helps pupils to understand the complexity of people's lives, the process of change, the diversity of societies and relationships between different groups, as well as their own identity and the challenges of their time.

This is a direct quote from the national curriculum on history. To understand and implement this we must consider the act of children's deeper learning and how it links to school and national curriculums and how to challenge and support children in their learning. Children's work in history should lend them skills which can be applied in other areas of their life, both personal, social and educational. In order for any history work to be worthwhile, educators and children must have high expectations of their achievements with the knowledge and expertise to develop and support their emergence as historians.

Creating an engaging, wholesome and intriguing schoolwide approach to history is a key factor in ensuring children get the most out of their topic studies and can meet the objectives outlined by the National Curriculum. Using the national curriculum to create an in school corporate approach to the teaching and learning of history will help to create and reach milestone targets, and assess progression and attainment against these. Every child has the ability to be a historian and many, in fact, are without realising. Any child that is curious about the history of their family or school has already taken that first step. It is our role to nurture this and help them develop further.

At the first stage of learning, children should begin to explore the meaning of yesterday, today, tomorrow and the concept of past, present and future. Children might be asked to describe what happened yesterday and arrange a timeline. This may be something as simple as a timeline of the events of the school day, their morning routine or recount something that happened in the past to the group. As children develop their learning, the timeline activity can become more complicated and more challenging concepts can be explored.

Timelines are something children in year one can complete easily but too often we see this repeated year after year without change. Asking nothing more demanding of children year after year limits their chance to progress and can be quite disengaging. Naturally, this becomes tiresome and does not produce a deeper learning or ability to relate periods in history to other events. A good way to extend this to create a deeper understanding is to have a timeline with two different series of events, especially if one of these is the history topic they studied last year or last term. When these are completed together it shows how their current topic relates to history in other areas of the world during the same period.

For example the sinking of Henry VIII's flagship *Mary Rose,* the European Colonisation of America and the Spanish Armada all occurred within seventy years of each other. During the defeat of the Aztec empire by Cortez and the occupation of Tenochtitlan, Magellan was discovering new lands and King Henry VIII sat the throne of England but these facts are rarely explored as taking place in the same period. Links between actions across the world are also rarely explored and the term chain reaction is often missed from many history lessons where it should be included. A good example of a chain reaction is the fact that World War One was partially caused by a driver taking a wrong turn and partially caused by worldwide colonialism, strange bedfellows indeed.

The national curriculum for history aims to ensure that all pupils:

- Know and understand the history of these islands as a coherent, chronological narrative, from the earliest times to the present day: how people's lives have shaped this nation and how Britain has influenced and been influenced by the wider world. *--A noble aim and one which must not be tainted by accidental imperialism or nationalism. The teaching must always seek to be factual and not opinionated. Certainly, advantages and disadvantages of empire for all peoples should be considered. The British Empire for example was a huge influence on the world and brought technology and medicine to areas that had never experienced them. But they also brought taxation, forced labour, slavery and new illnesses not to mention laws, customs and religion that was not* *native to the area. A good link here would be British values such as democracy and rule of law.*

- Know and understand significant aspects of the history of the wider world: the nature of ancient civilisations; the expansion and dissolution of empires; characteristic features of past non-European societies; achievements and follies of mankind. -- *Resources for this aim can sometimes be difficult to find at first glance but this can relate to the Romans, Ancient Greeks and Hellenistic era, Ancient Egypt and Aztecs and comparisons can be drawn between them such as the length of their existence, conquering of nearby nations, their impact on the modern world, their place in history and their fall or dissolution.*

- Gain and deploy a historically grounded understanding of abstract terms such as 'empire', 'civilisation', 'parliament' and 'peasantry'. -- *This can be worked into literacy work but finding and copying out a definition from the dictionary should only be part of understanding these concepts. Children should be able to explain the difference between a parliament under a Constitutional Monarchy or pre English Civil war monarchy and its role and the role of the Senate in the Roman Republic, a dictatorship such as Nazi Germany During the late 1930's and World War Two. Feudalism and the changing definition of peasantry through Norman to Post Medieval Britain, especially after events such as the Peasants Revolt/Rebellion (1381) and Black Death (c.1350) should also be examined closely to ensure a greater depth of understanding than 'peasants were poor people'.*

- Understand historical concepts such as continuity and change, cause and consequence, similarity, difference and significance, and use them to make connections, draw contrasts, analyse trends, frame historically-valid questions and create their own structured accounts, including written narratives and analyses. -- *This aim can be met by comparing different historical eras and approaches to their way of life such as the Paleolithic, Mesolithic and Neolithic periods of the Stone Age and the transition into the bronze age and the significance of the technology of metalworking. Working to understand what led to the changes in the way these prehistoric people lived and what influenced this. Questions such as 'Why did Stone Age people migrate? Where did they go? Why did they stop migrating? How did the bronze age come about? How did the use of bronze impact their lives?' are all valid questions to explore the topic. Enabling children to ask similar questions or these questions themselves can help achieve this aim, especially when children are able to find the answers to these questions through their own work and research.*

- Understand the methods of historical enquiry, including how evidence is used rigorously to make historical claims, and discern how and why contrasting arguments and interpretations of the past have been constructed. -- *Methods of inquiry and evidence in this aim should also include discussions of evidence and can we trust it, is it reliable? The use of terms such as primary source, secondary source, and terms such as biased, snapshot and propaganda should also be discussed and how these relate to each other. A good example of meeting this aim is studying the portrait of Elizabeth I after the defeat of the Spanish Armada and the imagery used to convey her power (hand on the globe) and the defeat of the Spanish (fire ships in background) and how this was not only a piece of propaganda but also a form of record of the battle. Conversations about the education of the general public, modern day fake news, and the unearthing of new evidence should also be a foundation part of this aim.*

- Gain historical perspective by placing their growing knowledge into different contexts, understanding the connections between local, regional, national and international history; between cultural, economic, military, political, religious and social history; and between short- and long-term timescales. -- *This aim is about linking the topic to the world stage as well as the typical local and national levels. For example if studying the local area close to Whitby the link may be the discoveries of Captain James Cook and how this influenced trade, military acts, justice, education, food, cartography, and our understanding of the world we live in. Another excellent example of this aim in real world history is the assassination of Arch Duke Franz Ferdinand. The killing of this one man in a relatively small country was the flashpoint for a domino effect of declarations of war across the world. Connecting a local event such as the first passenger railway and Locomotion Number One to the revolutionization of transport across the entirety of the*

North East creating a coal mining, factory and ship building economy and making Britain a trade empire to a worldwide network of logistics is a large but possible and definable leap. Timelines showing local, regional, national and worldwide events across a period of history are a good way to show this. Children should be able to relate to and explain how one historical event or period impacts the world. A leads to B, leads to C is a simple view of this and it should be explained with A caused B and also started a reaction leading to C, B and C combined caused D. These events happening meant that E had no option other than to action F. If A had not happened it is unlikely/more likely that the end result would have been the same.

When choosing your school or year group history curriculum and deciding which statutory and non-statutory subject content to study there is a lot to consider. Although the curriculum outlines that children should understand and be taught chronologically and using common historical terms there is more than simple A to B teaching. You must consider what resources the school already has available. For example if the school has previously studied Ancient Egypt a great deal there will likely be a wealth of on hand resources and subject knowledge from school staff.

Similarly if the school is situated close to areas that are closely linked to Roman Britain this should be utilised as being part of children's links to local as well as regional and national history, especially if the Roman settlements are parts of Britain's wider history such as Hadrian's Wall. If new resources would need to be sourced for a change in topic will the school budget account for this? This is a difficult question but must be considered. Difficulties can arise when trying to teach a topic when the only available resources are slideshows and staff knowledge and experience of the subject content is lacking. If changes do take place staff should be given plenty of notice to ensure they can plan appropriately and ask for resources.

Be mindful that mixed year groups or alterations in the period of history being taught will impact what should be chosen as there may be a crossover where some children will have experienced the work already. Obviously, this cannot happen as it will mean teaching a unit twice, therefore it is always important to know what other teachers in the school will be teaching and discuss this with each other to ensure history is being taught in a sensible and comprehensive way without causing friction between staff or repeating work.

The national history curriculum can be found here
https://assets.publishing.service.gov.uk/government/uploads/system/uploads/attachment_data/file/239035/PRIMARY_national_curriculum_-_History.pdf

Your school's history/humanities policy and curriculum interpretation should be updated every time there is a change in the relevant area of the national curriculum. It should also be evaluated as a staff team every three to five years at least, to ensure the school is still providing a high standard of education in this area, including offering the chance to expand the cultural capital of all pupils and to check the school approach to history in line with the school improvement plan. More regular evaluations may be necessary.

Cultural capital is something many children, especially disadvantaged children, can lack. It is the cultural experiences of British history, politics, music, monuments and structures that create the cultural experience of Britain. This can be the chance to visit cathedrals, abbeys, museums and castles. To listen to historical examples of music and taste and make historical food or experience non mainstream examples of these things. The cultural capital that can be offered by the study and proper use of resources for history is immense and should not be missed. Many of the resources and advice in this book can help bestow the cultural capital that may not otherwise be afforded to children.

Sometimes schools assume that children will have heard, seen, visited or otherwise experienced culturally significant participation. Even in well off areas children can often miss a great deal of cultural significance and have little to no opportunity of exploring the country and community they are a part of. Schools should seek to provide all children the opportunity to fulfil their cultural experiences even in areas where families are seen as well off as families in well off areas can be 'smokescreened'.

During your history work your children should become accustomed to the use of historical terms and tense sensitive language throughout the teaching of history. Specific lessons on the meaning of these words should be kept to a minimum as true understanding of these terms comes from class discussion and immersion in the terms. For each year group these are a suggested list that children should be able to use accurately and explain by the end of the school year.

Articulation of these words will improve as children age and improve their understanding. Simple explanations of words are acceptable until they have a strong understanding of everyday vocabulary and are able to comprehend more detailed explanations. Challenging terms and explanations do not need to be avoided as having a high expectation of children leads to excellent outcomes.

Below is a suggested list of words that children should be immersed in and be able to use accurately in a historical context. Children should also be able to explain the meaning of these words.

Foundation/Reception
- Today, yesterday, tomorrow, the past, the present, the future, day, week, month, year, old, new, a long time ago, remember, lifetime, calendar, material, age, young.

Year 1 (Including the previous list)
- Decade, century, fortnight, ancient, modern, timeline, in order of date, different, similar, inventions, famous, what, when, where, who, how, why, artefact, history.

Year 2 (including previous lists)
- Chronology/chronological order, era, millenia, diary, impact, significant, research, evidence, fact, opinion, tens, hundreds, thousands.

Year 3 (including previous lists)
- Period, source, prehistoric, records, debate, biased, BC (Before Christ), AD (Anno Domini), emperor, empire, republic, monarch, archaeologist, archaeology, proof, explain, describe, myth, legend,

fiction, written history, oral history, unexplained, first hand, second hand, change.

Year 4 (including previous lists)
- BCE, CE, invasion, civilisation, religious, covert, freedom, barbarian, legacy, culture, infer, suggest, expect, conclusion, cause, effect, impact.

Year 5 (including previous lists)
- Nation, region, local, world, turning point, reform, law, consequences, summary, similar/different, trade, economy, military, power, tradition, chain reaction.

Year 6 (including previous lists)
- Primary source, secondary source, biased view, promotion, position, influence, error, experiment, suggests, does not show, snapshot, flashpoint, insult, represent, attitude, freedom, rebellion, government, pre/post, propaganda, aristocracy, class, race, credible, unreliable, one sided, contrast, compare, personal, public.

Towards the end of a topic aim for the children to be able to accurately articulate the following:

1. The chronology of events.
2. Why events occurred.
3. Where they occurred.
4. Who was involved.
5. What was the impact of the event.
6. How does this link with other events at the time.
7. What they enjoyed learning about.

8. How else they could learn more on this topic.
9. How this topic could have been improved.

Your own language whilst teaching the history topic should seek to incorporate these terms in order that children become accustomed to using them in general discussion about history. Ensure there is opportunity for pupils to ask questions on the meanings of words and try to include a vocabulary sentence or word at least once a day.

A good starter activity is to choose one word from the list e.g. consequences, and then use this to find how many other words are hidden inside in one minute or write as many sentences with it in five minutes. A vocabulary sentence can be used to begin or end a lesson and can be located on a worksheet or children can write them in their books. 'Chronological means in order of time.' Is an example of a vocabulary sentence though lessons wholly on vocabulary can be useful but should not be overdone. A 'word of the day' starter or finishing activity can take all of thirty seconds and can be useful to promote the understanding of historical language.

It may be worth creating a question grid, such as the one below, in order to help children to create and ask questions to aid their understanding of history. The one below is a basic example which can be given to children so they are able to formulate questions and then tick the box once they have used the combination at least once. In this way we support children who struggle thinking of questions and help further children who may have lots of ideas but struggle to organise them efficiently. You may choose to create your own adaptation for a specific year group or topic with more limited or specific options.

Question Grid

	Who	What	When	Where	Why	How	Which
did							
is				X			
are							
will							
do							X
can							
does							
would							
might							
will						X	
did							

X= **Where is** the evidence for this?
X= **Which** source **do** we look at to get this information?
X= **How will** we prove this?

You should always endeavour to enable children to learn beyond the end of the topic. Consider providing some of the links and resources you find in this book to children and adults at home so they can continue exploring history in their own way. Many children have access to a tablet, computer or phone and can watch videos or browse the internet so exploit this and include parents and carers in the learning process. Do not assume that this is true however and try to provide alternatives, such as paper based work, for students that cannot access these resources or other alternatives to enable their learning.

https://www.history.org.uk/primary/categories/curriculum
This is useful for supporting your teaching of the curriculum. Remember that being a teacher does not mean you have to create and find every resource on your own. Whilst writing this book I asked the advice of my partner on matters of grammar and punctuation and for other experts in the field for their advice on content including history teachers, lecturers and children that both enjoy and dislike history as a subject. I also spoke with other authors who have written similar books and checked government and curriculum guidance.

Assessing children's learning in the area of history is important to ensure the teaching of the subject content and critical skills is working. Assessment should be used to;

A) Ensure children understand the content of the topic.

B) Ensure children are developing critical thinking skills.

C) Ensure children are developing investigative skills.

D) Identify where support should be implemented.

E) Ensure teaching is outstanding.

Assessment should be done primarily by the teacher and then only when necessary. With staff under heavy workload as is, there is no call for increasing this unduly. Below I have attached an assessment sheet that can be used for a class wide assessment. This can be adapted for each individual need but can be used as a whole class assessment against the timescaled objectives and identify areas to develop and where to target support.

<u>History Assessment</u>

<u>Class:</u>_____
<u>Teacher:</u>_____
<u>Time Period:</u>_____
Term 2 Week 3

<u>Objectives</u>	<u>Beginning</u>	<u>Expected</u>	<u>Secure</u>
Can identify how trustworthy a source of information is and explain why.	Aarron Aarronson, Barry Barryson, Colin Colinson	Daniel Danielson, Emma Emmason, Francis Francison	Garry Garryson

Can use year expectation history vocabulary accurately.	Aarron Aarronson	Barry Barryson, Colin Colinson, Daniel Danielson, Francis Francison	Garry Garryson, Emma Emmason
Overall Term 1	Aarron Aarronson	Barry Barryson, Colin Colinson, Daniel Danielson, Francis Francison	Garry Garryson
Action plan: Target support for AA, BB and CC. Provide vocabulary help sheets for AA. Create extension for GG,EE. Ensure differentiation is appropriate.			

Areas for development:
_____
_____
_____
_____

Areas for support:
_____
_____
_____

From this assessment we can see that Aarron Aarronson will need support, we can also see that Garry Garryson will need further development. If a large number of children are at either end of the scale, the work will need a general increase or decrease in challenge and differentiation will need to be altered. This assessment can also aid in targeting differentiation of work to help children reach their full potential and can also be used to show progression as children move from one box to another which can be evidenced with their work. This form of assessment should only be employed with the agreement of the school history lead to ensure a schoolwide approach. Children may begin in the first box in term one, week one and progress onwards.

Introducing a topic

The introduction of a topic should always seek to engage and excite the children. This is when teachers must become actors and comedians in order to sell the topic. Although this seems a crude phrase, we must seek to present the topic in a positive light even if it is a topic that does not particularly appeal to ourselves. An introduction of a topic should never rely solely on a slideshow. The slideshow should be for visual learners only and you should work to spark the children's imagination with your own inventive methods. For the purposes of this section we will assume we are teaching a topic on Roman Britain.

An example of introducing a topic is to create a slideshow with the topic title and a relevant background picture. Next, you will talk through some of the fantastic activities you will be doing together as a class with another slide to illustrate these points. This is your chance to promote the topic to the children. This is when you can generate the first interest in the topic and start the topic with a high level of engagement.

Lessons you may have planned may include creating a Roman oil lamp (link to art and DT framework), interviewing a real Roman/Celt (drama/speaking and listening/ creating, asking and answering questions using historical language.), creating a mosaic (art and DT framework), tasting/ making Roman food and writing a restaurant review/ letter of complaint (link to literacy and DT). Becoming Roman soldiers by making their armour and weapons then throwing javelins, marching together and running like a legionary (link to PE and DT.).

Naturally some lessons will be the 'boring' lessons of timelines, discussions on how Roman Britain linked to the rest of the world, cut and stick activities, sorting and comparing. Although these are not traditionally fun lessons they can still be extremely engaging and interesting if presented with enthusiasm and positive reinforcement of participation and these activities are broken up with the more energetic activities.

During your introduction of the topic you must ensure you are enthusiastic and confident to promote interest. This is a session which should not be left to other staff to cover such as during a PPA session as you will be the main lead of the topic and should introduce the topic to keep a stable base for future learning. By doing this children will feel confident that the lessons will be worthwhile and valuable whereas some covered lessons can be viewed as less important by children. Although this is not true it is the way children, especially older children, think. Later, it may be worthwhile involving other staff especially for dramatisations or other support. Consider a theme day during the topic and encourage children and staff to dress up like people from the period for the topic day and dedicate the full day towards the topic.

Communicating the topic and it's goals to adults at home recognises their part as being key educators of the children and can lead to adults supporting the children in the topic at home. Home learning can sometimes be more effective than school learning in some respects as home can offer a wider range of off curricular history such as documentaries and films or visits to areas of historical significance such as the Tower of London which would be difficult, or impossible, for the school to visit or utilise effectively. Involving the home in the introduction of the topic is for the benefit of all and helps foster a relationship of mutual respect and support of a child's learning.

During your introduction to the topic ensure it is planned for a day when there are few distractions. Children should not be absent from the introduction as they miss the prospects of the topic they are immediately disengaged from the learning because they do not know what to expect. Due to the busy nature of a school day with children leaving the room for interventions, occupational therapy, physiotherapy, speech and language, social skills sessions, music lessons, school council meetings, police cadets etc etc etc, there is no easy way to plan this.

History will never hold the same status as Literacy, Numeracy and ICT in schools but this does not mean it should be dismissed out of hand as a subject that is not important. To do so means that you have already failed in your responsibility to teach history and ensure the mistakes of the past are not forgotten.

The First Step

A journey of a thousand miles begins with a single step. For a first session it is always worthwhile to give a broad overview to the topic (see previous chapter) in a way which is both interesting and exciting. A good way to do this is via online videos such as the Simple History Youtube channel or making a short powerpoint. Note, pre-made powerpoints and videos such as those from teaching resource websites can often contain outdated or irrelevant information and these should be checked before use. After an introduction and explanation of the topic you should ask your children to make a mind map showing the following.

1. What they already know about Roman Britain. (or whichever topic.)
2. What they would like to find out about Roman Britain.

3. How they can find this out.
4. When they will find out these things.
5. Any experiences they have with Roman Britain e.g. visiting Hadrian's Wall, seeing a re-enactment, seeing Roman exhibits in museums etc.

Once this activity has been completed you will be able to see the different range of prior knowledge the children already have in this area and the most popular things they want to learn about. In my experience, children want to learn about the Roman Army more than anything else to do with the Romans. From here you can use this to influence your planning for related lessons and activities. From this point you can also discuss the different ways children can discover this information. Promote related reading books, documentaries or places to visit such as Vindolanda or Chedworth Roman Villa.

A similar activity to this can round up the topic by detailing what they have learned, how they learned it, the most interesting fact they discovered and how they would improve the topic next time. Incorporate the results from this work into your planning, home learning and end of topic targets to ensure children reach their full potential and achieve their own targets of discovering facts. Involving children in the planning process of their own learning helps them gain control of their education and feel their opinions and interests are valued and considered. This will also help children to feel engaged as they are taking an active role and are empowered in their learning.

Now the topic has properly begun you must keep up your enthusiasm and flare to deliver your history topic. Often children enjoy the disgusting and weird bits of history and children should be exposed to these as appropriate for their age. When studying the religions of historical civilisations you can often find oddities that modern people consider funny. The Romans for example had a goddess of door hinges and handles named Cardea. Including funny oddities such as this alongside your usual teaching helps keep lessons fresh and interesting and a few of these thrown in to your first session or two will help ignite keenness in returning to the topic.

Facts such as Cleopatra was actually of Greek descent not Egyptian, Caligula loved his horse so much he gave him his own servants, and the Vikings discovered America, are all facts which will keep the topic in the mind of your pupils. Making a topic fun is not only about including interesting information but doing it in a way which makes it relevant, accessible and memorable. What made Horrible Histories so popular was that it did not try to shield children from the gruesome, hilarious and depressing parts of history but allowed them to explore them in a fun and engaging way full of fun tidbits, quizzes and well presented content. Horrible Histories books should be available in the school for children to read. I would also suggest that anybody wishing to teach history should read the books relating to their topics at the very least.

Drama

An excellent tool in the armoury of teaching topic work is drama. I, and many other educators have used this most successfully in order to generate passion for the work amongst children and get the most out of their learning, but it does require some knowledge, confidence and an ability to think on your feet. One possible drama use is for an interview with a historical figure. The way this activity works is that you advertise to the children that they will interview a real life Roman Soldier/ Viking Warrior/ Captain Cook/ Florence Nightingale/ Mary Seacole/ Amelia Earhart. What you do next is ask the children to create questions to ask the 'Time Traveller'. It is best to stick with open ended questioning here to attempt to get the most from the interview though some closed questions can be acceptable.

For the actual interview a member of staff, or a visitor if available, needs to dress up and act as the person to be interviewed. For this activity it is best to form a link with a local re-enactment group who can visit the school or use video conference technology.

http://www.upanatemhistory.com/
This is a first rate group to consider for this kind of activity. Another superb group for the study of the World War's is the Remembering Tommy school visit re-enactors. These can be found on Facebook under the name Remembering Tommy which I have linked below. The person dressing up and playing the role of the interviewee must have a good knowledge of the subject and will need to have a look at some of the questions beforehand to ensure they can answer anything that is asked. The costume should be as accurate as possible but naturally it is not possible to spend a few hundred pounds on an accurate outfit as staff so something as close as possible is best. Simply look up the character and attempt to get an outfit as close as you can if going with the staff member as an interviewee route. If you know a re-enactor, are working with a museum or are in contact with a re-enactment group they will be able to take the role of the interviewee, though there may be some cost associated.

Many museums have loan boxes which may contain historical costumes and artefacts that can be borrowed for free. If neither of these appeal to you there is always the option of putting a sewing machine to good use to create a costume from scratch. Make sure you research what it should look like before you begin.

Typically the activity begins with the character entering the classroom whilst the children are already sat down but the character can also be in the room as they enter though this can mean they take longer to settle. The character should stay in the role for the entire interview and deny all knowledge of being someone else until the session is over. Children with SEN, particularly ASC, can sometimes find this unnerving and may need to be reassured that it is in fact a normal person who has only dressed up to speak to them. If SEN children become distressed they should be escorted to a quiet/mental health well being space by a member of staff.

Other drama roles can include hotseating of children as they answer questions as though they were a character, parliament or debate sessions where children argue for and against a statement such as should the Stone Age people use stone tools or switch to bronze, though some preparation work on the pros and cons of this should have been done beforehand.

http://www.bbbpress.com/dramagames/
This is a list of drama activities you can adapt for history links.

https://www.ebay.co.uk/itm/Roman-Lorica-Segmentata-Armor-Breastplate-Costume-Brass-Lined-Segmenta/292822252111?hash=item442d90fa4f:g:PHcAAOSwUfVb8TVN
This is a link for full size Roman armour. Useful for display and interviews. A great many costumes can be found online, though not always perfectly accurate.

https://www.facebook.com/rememberingtommyatkins/

A superb example of the fantastic re-enactors that can visit schools for drama work. I would highly recommend this as both cost effective and superb for children's learning.

This is an excellent article on when not to recreate history through drama experience.
https://www.cultofpedagogy.com/classroom-simulations/

Food

Making and eating food as a part of your history topic is a great way to get a glimpse into the past. Whether making hard tack, stews, biscuits or trench cakes the creation and tasting of food brings a new dynamic to the school day. It is fairly straightforward to find historical recipes with a quick internet search. Obviously, the food technology will be limited by what it is safe and possible to do in school and you should not try to overextend what is practical otherwise the activity may be a write off. Stews will require hobs or hot plates, biscuits and breads need ovens.

There are no cook recipes such as cakes and cold foods such as fruits and cheeses. This might be a good opportunity to teach about the impact food had on history and how technology changed with the need for more food for a larger population. Migration of peoples in the Stone Age or rationing during the World Wars. There is a wide variety of food that can be created and is inclusive for those that have special dietary needs such as diabetes, gluten intolerance, wheat, fruit and fructose difficulties. Below I will list a recipe for hardtack biscuits along with a description of their usage.

You must check children's allergies and food intolerances before undertaking any recipes.

Hard tack biscuits are made primarily from flour, salt and water. They last a long time without going mouldy and as such were great for journeys of long distance or when food was difficult to source such as in the Age of Sail and during the World Wars. The problem with them was that they would often be full of weevils after a while, they are also extremely hard to eat and often were broken up and soaked in tea, alcohol or soup before they were eaten. (Be aware they are extremely hard.) These were in use from the age of sail right up until post World War Two. Captain Cook and the men in the trenches of the First World War will have eaten much the same in the form of hardtack.

You will need:

- 1 lb flour
- ½ pint of water, or milk for a softer biscuit
- ½ tablespoon salt

- 2 oz butter for a softer biscuit

1. Preheat the oven to 180.
2. Grease baking tray.
3. Wash hands and dry.
4. Mix flour and salt in a mixing bowl.
5. Melt butter into the milk on low heat in a saucepan until completely melted.
6. Add milk and butter (or just use water) and mix until a dough is formed.
7. Roll the dough out until between 1cm and 2 cm thick.
8. Cut using a cup rim. Do not twist.
9. Re-roll dough and repeat.
10. Place on a greased baking tray and prick twice with a fork. (The more they are pricked the harder they will be.)
11. Bake at 180 until golden brown.
12. Leave to cool.

WARNING - these biscuits are extremely hard if done to the original recipe.

You may notice this is the same recipe for making salt dough christmas ornaments. You may be put off by this and for good reason. They taste ok, sort of like an incredibly dense, incredibly hard cracker that may break your teeth. Make some for yourself and try them but you have been warned. For a frontline soldiers meal during WW2 add corned beef or spam, a square of chocolate, some processed cheese, tea, vegetable stew, dried fruit, jam and porridge. Mix and match to create a meal or try some home front cooking such as potato peel pie, Woolton pie, bread pudding or eggless cake.

A good list of WW2 recipes can be found here.
https://the1940sexperiment.com/100-wartime-recipes/

For an even more in depth experience create a school vegetable garden and explain that in the past a lot of food had to be home grown. Maintain this throughout the year and then eat when in season in a recipe from the topic. An orienteering challenge could work with children collecting ingredients or recipe cards at each marker and then create a meal with what they have collected. This activity will promote teamwork and links well with most historical food lessons, especially Stone Age food due to their survival as a hunter gatherer society.

http://cookit.e2bn.org/
This as a fantastic website containing many historical recipes.

When teaching be careful not to fall into the trap of misunderstanding evidence. Evidence shows that rich Tudor houses spent a lot of money on buying meat, alcohol, spices, sweet food and luxuries but little to no money was spent on fruit and vegetables. Many teachers explain that this is because they did not eat these in their diets. This is not true. If you are a Tudor landowner you will likely have people working some of your land growing fruit and vegetables. If you grow your own vegetables you are unlikely to spend a lot of money on buying it from other local farms. Similarly most rich Tudors had an orchard or at least sent people to pick from wild fruit in the forests and fields or hawthorn leaves.

It's a common misconception that the evidence backs up the first theory but this does not take into account evidence of human remains showing their diets to contain fruit and vegetables and both graphical and literary descriptions of kitchens and cooking in the era to understand diets amongst the rich were better than first thought. Don't worry if you have taught children this in the past, never be afraid to admit you don't know something about history or that you have made a mistake. Explain that you will, or have, researched it and will come back with an answer. This will promote the idea of doing your own research and continuing your own historical learning to the children and reinforces that it is ok to not be an expert on everything and that making mistakes is how we learn.

Displaying and comparing the tools, utensils and household items that were used in the procurement, production, preparation, cooking and eating of food can also be an important factor of exploring history. Finding and eating food in the Stone Age was a great deal more difficult than boiling a kettle and filling a noodle pot with boiling water. At one educational visit I accompanied we saw a historic kitchen complete with ovens, open fireplace, copper kettles and pans, long wooden trestle tables, mortars and pestles and other equipment I could not hazard a guess at. The children were amazed to find there was no microwave and no quick fixes like crisps or chocolate bars. Beyond their own home they had never seen the way people in the past had created food, the only comparison they were able to draw was that one of their grandmothers had an aga in their home.

http://www.foodtimeline.org/ This is an excellent resource to find where our earliest records of food come from and when they have been dated.

https://www.historic-uk.com/CultureUK/History-of-British-Food/ Another useful site with a focus on British food.

http://www.pompeiitaly.org/en/food-drink/the-typical-dishes-of-ancient-pompeii/
Here you can find information on Roman food from Pompeii. Be sure to look up a picture of the bread preserved in the eruption of Mount Vesuvius.

http://www.localhistories.org/food.html
A superb link for a basic overview of food and dining in history.

https://www.reddit.com/r/Old_Recipes/
A media page full of old recipes from users. Includes recipe and finished product in some cases.

Educational Visits

A school trip to a museum or historically significant site is an excellent way to engage young minds with history. Superb examples exist across Britain of visitable areas to promote the teaching of history. Beamish Living Museum of the North, Vindolanda, Raby Castle, RAF Hendon, Yorkshire Air Museum, The National Museum of the Royal Navy, Historic Town of Bath, International Bomber Command Centre Lincoln, York and the Jarvik centre and Whitby are just some examples. Many museums such as Head of Steam Darlington offer reduced or free visits for schools and these should be taken advantage of at every opportunity.

Encourage children to interact safely with the site. Some attractions have interactive displays or staff present to create a more in depth learning opportunity. Remember your role on a trip is not always to be the learning leader but rather a safe point of contact for children to be around whilst learning through play and appropriate risk via exploration. It may be a good idea to split up into smaller groups with staff and explore a smaller area with say, six children, before moving onto another area.

Educational trips to relevant historical areas can be stand alone, end of year or part of a larger trip. Even a fleeting visit to a historical site as part of a bigger expedition is useful. Seeing a castle and standing in the barbican or beside a curtain wall gives a good impression of the power and permanence it emanated. Even splitting a trip between two different places can be useful such as visiting Raby Castle and Barnard Castle on the same day to compare and contrast. The most memorable trip for myself was Eden Camp which seemed to go on forever and provided a superb experience. This was a trip repeated once a year by the school and always proved popular. Some visits may not be age appropriate or safe for children and if possible two staff members should visit beforehand to perform a risk assessment and scout the site.

Beamish Museum offers two staff tickets for free before the visit to ensure the school has opportunity to accurately assess the risk. Continuation activities should be planned to follow up on the excursion to maximise the potential of the experience.

Take plenty of photos and as always set a limit of between £5-£15 of spending money to be brought. I will never forget the child who wanted to buy a pencil with a £50 note. Post-trip photos and activities should be used on a display or website to keep adults at home involved.

Due to budget restrictions we must be realistic and understand that an educational history trip is not a main priority. In this instance I would suggest turning your classroom into something from the topic. With some cardboard, craft materials and crepe paper your classroom can become a castle with a medieval teacher of HM Bark Endeavour. Although this is a high effort project it can be extremely rewarding for the children and they will always remember the day their classroom was transported through time. However, some attractions such as the National Museum of Scotland and the National Portrait Gallery of Scotland are free entry and will require only the cost of transport, often such visits must be pre-booked and slots can be difficult to source.

http://www.redspottedhanky.com/destination-guides/adventure/best-free-museums-in-the-uk/
This link has some suggestions for free museum visits.
https://www.historic-uk.com/Blog/Top-10-Historical-Sites-in-the-UK/
A great link for suggested visits. Some will not be applicable to your school.

http://www.beamish.org.uk/learning/plan-your-school-visit/
A link to Beamish Museum, a living history museum with multiple eras to visit.

Remember to take plenty of photos!

Subject Knowledge

Subject knowledge in history is just as important as it is in mathematics. Teaching children that 5+5=11 is just as bad as teaching children that the Romans vomited during meals so they could eat more. The word vomitorium, from which this is derived, is in fact the entrance and exit to a stadium. Far too often I have been to a school only to see work which is full of inaccuracies that the teacher has marked correct.

Unfortunately some teachers refuse to admit updated guidance and resources are in fact correct and cling onto old methods. An example of this is the resting place of Richard III of England of the House of York. Even today, eight years after his remains were discovered in a car park in Leicester, some teachers still teach that his body was hacked apart at Bosworth and has never been found. In order to ensure your resources are accurate you must check that you are not stocking or displaying out of date resources on the subject and that you yourself check the content of what you are teaching.

There is no excuse for teaching incorrect information, it would not be acceptable to teach the incorrect placements of full stops and neither is it acceptable to teach history incorrectly. There are a great number of Youtube channels with information across a range of history subjects, as I have previously addressed, Simple History is superb for an overview of a topic.

As I have already mentioned it is important to ensure your subject matter is up to date so check the dates of the videos for relevancy. Steer clear from historically inaccurate films or film clips as a way of teaching except for the purposes of dramatisations. For a historical review on films search History Buffs on Youtube, this channel reviews the accuracy of history films and is widely trusted as a useful measure of the films quality. If you would like to take a short course on history they can often be found in local areas as summer university courses, community interest courses or here
https://www.futurelearn.com/subjects/history-courses.

I understand that you may not be particularly interested in history. You yourself may find it to be a boring subject or you may find it difficult to teach. Every teacher has a subject they dread or a section of a subject that always escapes your interest or understanding, this is only natural so don't feel that you must enjoy every topic. For me this is the Ancient Egyptians. I find it to be poorly structured, difficult to understand and spread over such a huge timeline that I routinely get confused as to whether I'm talking of Ramses, Tutankhamun or Ptolemy. Despite this I try to teach it in the best way possible and hide my displeasure at this topic.

https://www.youtube.com/channel/UC510QYlOIKNyhy_zdQxnGYw
This is useful for giving yourself a basic overview of a topic or event.

https://www.youtube.com/channel/UC88lvyJe7aHZmcvzvubDFRg
These documentaries are useful for your own knowledge.

When expanding your own subject knowledge, find an area you like and learn what you can from it, inevitably this will link to other areas. Rome links to Ancient Greece, Iron Age Britain, Egypt, and Hellenism. At the very bare minimum you should research the lessons you are going to teach, I have seen teachers stop a lesson part way through to check the answers or look up something they should have already checked and readily announce to the class that they didn't check the answers. This disengages the children and sends the message that it is not important to learn history. This sort of blunder would not be tolerated in other subjects or under observations so it should not be tolerated for a history lesson. Undertaking a work and planning scrutiny of history is an important part of ensuring subject content is correct. I hate work scrutinies, I always have done, but they can be useful to check history is being taught in a sensible way. In order for work scrutinies to work effectively the school must agree to a school wide teaching pattern for history so that pupils do not repeat topics, assessment is easily understood and that resources can be allocated effectively.

The work scrutiny should include the history lead, a member of the Senior Leadership Team and a member of staff of any grade that is specialised in history, this includes support staff and governors. Remember the point of this scrutiny is to ensure subject content is correct. These scrutinies on history should be limited to once per year at a maximum unless serious or reoccurring issues are evident. The point of these scrutinies is not to blame or find fault but to promote good historical practices. If there is a period of high workload, high stress or high disruption, work scrutiny should not go ahead except for those stated on the school improvement plan. The mental health of staff is worth more than a sudden burst of extra work.

Local Area

Your local area will always have a wealth of fascinating history. From smuggling on the coast to building the first passenger railway, Britain has an intensely rich history. Living in a country with recorded history stretching back almost 2000 years there are many areas to explore and mysteries to uncover. Most schools focus on the local area topic at one stage or another which can often show just how little children, parents and staff know of the area they live in. A good way to explore this, if it is safe to do so, is a walking tour of the local area. If a guide or person with historical knowledge of the area is able to accompany the trip there is a wealth of information to discover.

I have met children that had no idea there are plague pits in their village and others that had explored a Second World War era pillbox but had no idea of its purpose other than a canvas for graffiti. Often we walk through the areas we live in without considering that we are amongst and a part of history. Who has time to consider the building with the plaque on the front when we are late for work? Who has time to look up information on the old house converted into flats? Who can be bothered to cross the road to examine the out of place memorial? It is likely you have passed something with historical significance with nothing more than a cursory glance. We have lived through a worldwide pandemic, that is now history, as is our experience of it.

You can apply for a free copy of parish records to shed more light on the people who lived and worked in the local area, especially those that have lived there for a long time. Consider creating a family tree with your class and then trying to find drawings or photographs to compare how the place their parents and grandparents came from compares to the modern area. Put these together in a flip book along with photos of the local area to show how the place they live and learn in has changed with the additions of new housing estates, the closure of butchers, grocers and haberdasheries to pave the way for shopping centres and the addition of roads, airports and railway lines.

https://maps.nls.uk/geo/explore/side-by-side/#zoom=15&lat=54.51750&lon=-1.47407&layers=171&right=11 This is a site that shows side by side maps showing how areas have changed, it takes some time to find the area you are looking for but it offers a wonderful comparison. Do your best to involve staff, parents and local residents in order to teach this topic. Your local library may be able to offer a great deal of resources for this topic, librarians are often overlooked and undervalued sources of local history.

https://www.nationalarchives.gov.uk/help-with-your-research/research-guides/census-records/ This is a guide to finding, accessing and understanding census records.

Rewards and Extra Curricular Activities

Incorporating history into the reward charts of the classroom helps the topic become immersive. A class reward chart could become a picture of a Viking warrior and for each class award a section is coloured in. Once full, the class gets a party.

Individual reward charts could become a class of Roman soldiers sailing to Britain. The first person to fill their reward chart lands first and gets a sack of gold (chocolate) coins as a reward. There is a lot of scope for including history in the classroom and linking it to other areas, be as creative as you can. Consider awarding a history certificate for the best piece of history work of the term or have a 'historian of the week' display to reward children's hard work. During worker of the week or praise assembly be mindful that they are rarely awarded for work relating to history.

These should be used in conjunction with your usual behaviour management policies and should not replace them entirely. Naturally, any classroom behaviour management should be presented as a unified effort and all staff who work in the classroom should be made aware of and be able to use these behaviour management tools. This should include job share teachers, teaching assistants, cover supervisors, HLTA's and CSA's.

https://www.ebay.co.uk/itm/HISTORY-CHILDS-CHILDREN-TROPHY-KINGS-QUEENS-ENGRAVED-FREE-MINI-STAR-TROPHIES/401478914694?hash=item5d7a021286:g:fjIAAOSwMqBaYLqe
This is a link to a history trophy you could award for a particularly impressive project. I use these myself for extra-curricular history activities or for children that have consistently shown outstanding achievement in history.

Setting up an after school history club is an excellent way to involve more children in a more hands on history experience. Most after school clubs seem to be sport centred which leaves more academically inclined children with few choices.

In my experience of after school history clubs they are hugely successful, sometimes reaching sizes in excess of twenty or thirty attendees. Activities which may not fit into regular teaching time or subjects off of the national curriculum are always good choices for the after school club and it can also be a good idea to invite adults from home if the staff are happy to do this.

The extra curricular group can explore a topic or stand alone activities but it is essential that the staff running the club have a good knowledge of history and are able to impart it effectively. This does not mean they must be a teacher or even teaching assistant as I started an extra curricular history project when I was still a volunteer. Some of the activities undertaken in extracurricular opportunities would never have been able to go ahead in a typical school day due to demands such as space. I will list a few activities below and will also include a short activity plan as an example. Remember that the primary aim of this club was to create and nurture an interest in history.

- Fencing (led by a qualified instructor)
- Archery (Led by a local archery club)
- History of the RAF talk by a re-enactor in costume with props.
- Lifeboat activity (see PE section)
- Created Spitfires out of materials from home then voted on whose was best. (Winner took home an art set.)
- Multiple food tasting activities. (Age of sail, WW1, WW2, modern military rations, etc)
- 1940's PE style lesson including air raid.

- Family tree sessions with in school display of family photos with home adults permission.
- Visited a local museum with home adults. (Fee waived for children.)
- Handled artefacts and analysed them for markings and clues as to use and manufacture.
- Discussed our favourite history books, poems, films and TV shows.
- Video called an archaeologist.
- Created an in school art display of our family crest and our own new designs.
- Local history exploration.

Traditionally at the end of each term the children would vote for one amongst them who had distinguished themselves. The winner would then receive a trophy.

Extra Curricular History Club Planning

Resources: History club rewards located in lockable cupboard in BLANK Slideshow of session titles and rules.	**Task** Introduce topic. Outline sessions- How and why the Titanic disaster impacted the world so much. Discuss what we will be exploring. The building of the Titanic, the sinking, why rescue took so long and why so many lost their lives, the impact on maritime activities, modern myths, the Titanic now.
Objectives Introduce the topic. Discuss ground rules, e.g. no touching items until told to do so, no shouting out, respectfulness, more focus on fun interactive learning rather than learning my rote and text.	**Key questions** What would you like to learn about the Titanic? What rules would you like to institute? What do you already know about Titanic? How could we discover these things outside of schools?
For next session Next session we will look at the building and beginning of the maiden voyage of RMS Titanic.	**Special notes** BLANK suffers from BLANK and must have BLANK with them at all times.

Display

Display is often limited to two things. A display board with some of the children's work and a tabletop display of books and one or two artefacts. There is nothing wrong with this and these should be employed as the typical displays of the school but this can be improved upon. Be honest with yourself and ask how often does a display really grab your attention? After a few years they all blur into one.

For the price of £100 you can buy a full size set of armour on ebay, or sets of historical clothing or artefact boxes. If you can convince the school to front the cost, history can come alive. Instead of seeing everything in a book or on a screen suddenly there is a real set of armour in the classroom, real oil lamps and coins to handle. If this price is too high a miniature set of most armours can be bought for about half the price. Again on Ebay, reproduction battle dress from the Second World War can be found fairly cheaply. Most of this is replica and is useful for children to try on. Similarly helmets of Viking, Roman, World Wars and Medieval replicas can be found cheaply.

Although this would cost money and the school may not agree to pay they can be an amazing addition to your display. You can also buy replica coins, mosaic tiles, chainmail, drinking mugs, wooden bowls, arrowheads and more. Some for as cheap as £2. A great deal of interest can be created via displays, not just for the children in your class, but also other children and staff. Your usual displays should also be as interactive as possible as well as displaying children's work. Consider displaying period authentic adverts, toys, clothes or posters and photos. The more bright and eye catching your display the better. Be as creative as possible when creating your displays and don't be afraid to experiment. The more stunning they are the better, try to capture photographic evidence of completed displays for future reference or to include in evidence files when applying for jobs.

An interesting idea is to turn your display board into a large scale map and annotate with either a battle timeline or split the board into two or three sections, depending on size, and create a time lapse map. An effective idea to see this is the change in borders of the Roman Empire as it grew from town, to city state, to country, to empire. Displays in this form illustrate the change of time and can also be useful as a local area display in the same vein.

It may be a good idea to create a permanent box of display items for each topic. These can then be labelled and kept in the cupboard for when they are needed. This is a list of suggested resources to be kept in a 'quick topic box'. Having one of these boxes makes preparing for a topic much quicker and can support other teachers when they teach the topic.

- Age appropriate books. (Mix of fiction and non-fiction)
- Artefacts. (Coins, clothing, armour, weapons, tools, pictures of food, light sources, household items, local and world maps, documents, entertainment.)
- Posters.
- A file of last year's planning + work examples.
- USB drive of slideshows and useful links.
- Museum resources.
- Dressing up resources if applicable.

Below is a list of books that are suggested to be available in the school library or class reading area. In your class you should always provide books relating to the particular topic but some history books should always be present on your shelves. Remember to provide books for a range of reading abilities and interests.

- Encyclopedia of British History.
- Encyclopedia of World History.
- A Street Through Time.
- A City Through Time.
- What was it like in the past? (series)
- World Atlas/Globe
- Pre-Historic England.
- Who Am I? Family Tree Explorer.
- My First Book of Questions and Answers (Long Ago)
- History Year by Year.
- Take 10 Years Series.
- 100 Events That Made History.
- Amazing History Facts.
- Ladybird Histories.
- Horrible Histories.
- Children's History Atlas.
- Local area books.
- Age appropriate fiction books with a historical narrative e.g. Stone Age Boy, War Horse, Boy.

Each class should also have a timeline displayed. This can either relate to the topic, nation or world. It is possible to display all of these to show a link between them which can aid children in their understanding of the important events in history and how these relate to each other. If the same timeline is repeated throughout the school it will become a background to be ignored. An interesting concept is the use of an entire corridor mural to show the history of the school from its founding to the present day. Celebrating the history of your school is an important activity and should be undertaken as a whole school at least once a year.

https://instantdisplay.co.uk/otherhistory.html This is a useful link for history displays and many others besides.

http://www.aheadofhistory.co.uk/2017/10/classroom-displays-on-historical.html Some free printouts for history displays.

Partnerships

Developing partnerships with local museums and historians is always a step in the right direction for developing teaching of history. Try to form as many as possible by reaching out to see if there are any projects you can be a part of. Networking with others is a great opportunity to keep up to date with changes made to the teaching and learning of history across the country as well as keeping your own skills sharp. Discuss with your history lead how to best use the resources available from partnerships with your children.

https://teesvalleymuseums.org/ is a collection of museums that are working together to engage with audiences as a collective in the Tees Valley. Similar organisations exist across the UK, more information is usually available from your local museums.

https://historicengland.org.uk/ is a useful website especially for free historical photographs which can be found by area, date and genre.

https://www.english-heritage.org.uk/learn/school-visits/
English heritage allows school visits for free if they are led by school staff in an unguided tour. Guided tours are more informative but can be expensive, with a bit of homework and a pre-visit check you can save a bit of money and maybe learn something you didn't already know.

https://www.classtrips.co.uk/history-school-trips/

This is another useful website to see a list of recommended school trips related to history. Almost all museums offer free loan boxes to schools which are useful if a school trip is not feasible for whatever reason. Working with other schools can also help share history resources such as staff knowledge and experience and any personal collections they may have. Schools may be invited to take part in local projects out of the blue run by museums or history groups. These should be accepted if possible and not always managed by the history lead. I have managed many of these projects purely due to my experience in working alongside museums, this is a good example of using the expertise of school staff.

Engaging with youth groups outside of school can also benefit your children's education relating to history especially those that have rich history of their own such as Scouts or Guides. Your school can also work towards attaining heritage school status and the superb opportunities that accompany it. Building partnerships can require a lot of groundwork at the start but often leads to much better rewards for both sides after the hard work of establishing a connection.

Find more information on heritage schools here.
https://historicengland.org.uk/services-skills/education/heritage-schools/

You may also choose to speak to the history lead about attaining the History Quality Mark though there is some cost incurred. Find out more here
https://www.history.org.uk/primary/categories/quality-mark

Music

Music says things words can't and making or even listening to historical music can really give you a sense of being in the era. Background music during a lesson related to the subject can be quite useful to bring atmosphere into the room though some children find this difficult to cope with. A good example of this is simple gregorian chants whilst working or listening to a carnyx to hear the same sound Celts did before a battle. One good experiment is to split the class into two groups and direct them to create two pieces of music in a similar style to whatever period you are studying. One piece for a celebration and another for a sad occasion then compare to modern music for the same reasons. This can help draw a comparison between ancient and modern music.

https://www.youtube.com/watch?v=Bu9PyoiArys&t=48s&ab_channel=DaveMartel The wonderful sound of the Carnyx.

Here we have an example of some Native American chants. https://www.youtube.com/watch?v=W9HMB4ALAlg&ab_channel=Chamvideos
Native Americans are considered a Stone Age people along with many of the South American peoples.

https://www.youtube.com/results?search_query=hush+hush+hush+here+comes+the+boogeyman A lesser known song from WW2, not as popular as Vera Lynn or George Formby but a good example none-the-less.

Chants that may have been heard before the dissolution of the monasteries are useful for background music.
https://www.youtube.com/watch?v=VBgoU2M5J_s&ab_channel=ElsaMars

A Roman Cornu.
https://www.youtube.com/watch?v=1IlZgj2FAHA&ab_channel=AbrahamCupeiro

Stone Age instruments.
https://www.youtube.com/watch?v=qqKR_y0iDao&ab_channel=AshmoleanMuseum

Stone Age rock gongs.
https://www.youtube.com/watch?v=pW8h6PBTY-Q&ab_channel=LisaEspi

The oldest known melody
https://www.youtube.com/watch?v=QpxN2VXPMLc&ab_channel=DamianMusicChannel4

An evolution of music.
https://www.youtube.com/watch?v=oxRZwjVkPDo&ab_channel=ABAlphaBeta

Evolution of music 2.
https://www.youtube.com/watch?v=swQ1CvUShow&ab_channel=ABAlphaBeta

You may wish to play some 'bardcore' music. This is modern music played in a medieval style.

Famous People

When teaching about famous people an opportunity exists to broaden the horizons of children and tackle stereotypes. Famous people topics were, for a long time, usually focussed on middle and upper class white European men. I am pleased to say this has changed and a much wider range of figures are considered for this topic.

During discussions of famous people it is advisable to do some research on your own rather than rely solely on older resources as information about these people can change with time. It is also not a good idea to rely on popular culture such as films or TV as these are often dramaticised and condensed in order to fulfil the particular aims of those that stand to profit from the production and sale of these titles. When looking at famous people they should never be made out to be more than human, they will have both positive and negative character traits and to pretend otherwise is dishonest. An element of hero worship can creep into history work when discussing famous people and this should be balanced with honest and critical reviews on their other less wholesome traits.

Boudicca is often upheld as a fearless warrior who threw off the yoke of Roman oppression for her people. The fact that she contributed to the killing of civilians is glossed over. Concentration camps are almost always associated with Nazi Germany, but they exied in many other countries and time periods, including British Colonial Africa. I have used the following activity to challenge children's views of famous historical figures. This activity was designed and implemented with year 6 children but can be adapted.

Create a table with a list of famous people, these should be a mix of different genders, races and morals. My personal list contained Boudicca, Julius Caesar, Winston Churchill, Adolf Hitler, Martin Luther King Jr, Genghis Khan, Elizabeth I and Henry VIII. On one side write a good point about the person, on the other a bad then cut this up and distribute one copy each to a group of children. Ask them to match up the names and the good and bad points. It's fascinating to see children immediately assign every bad trait to Adolf Hitler and every good trait to those with English sounding names. It leads to an excellent discussion about bias and how history is influenced by the powerful and victorious.

This is a suggested list of famous people that may be beneficial to study.

- Mary Seacole
- Martin Luther King Jr
- Montgolfier Brothers
- Wright Brothers
- Thomas Eddison
- Tesla
- Boudicca
- Julius Caesar
- Guillaume of Normandy
- Genghis Khan
- Winston Churchill
- Elizabeth I
- Henry VIII
- Oliver Cromwell

- Napoleon Buonaparte
- William Shakespere.
- Queen Victoria
- Amy Johnson
- Captain James Cook
- Lewis Carroll
- Rosa Parks
- Barack Obama
- Margaret Thatcher
- Ignatius Sancho
- Sun Tzu
- Confucious
- Omar Khayyam
- Salladin
- George Washington
- Barack Obama
- Joad of Arc
- Gandhi
- Mother Teresa
- Nelson Mandela
- Arthur Wellesley
- William Wallace
- Robert De Brus
- Anne Frank
- Galileo
- Leonardo Da Vinci
- Richard III
- Madam C J Walker
- Cleopatra
- Marie Curie

This is not an exhaustive list and you should consult with your history lead or history team to decide on which historical figures best suit your needs. You may choose to select a local historical figure to study alongside or in place of a national or worldwide figure. Often a local figure can be easier for younger children to relate to as many of the locations or names may already be familiar with them, especially if their name or image is displayed in the town or possibly school.

https://www.brainpop.com/socialstudies/famoushistoricalfigures/ A useful website for the study of historical figures.

Experimental Archaeology

Experiments are not just reserved for science lessons and can be undertaken for history lessons with some preparation. Experimental archaeology is trying to live the experience of people from the time period in order to understand why or how certain things were done. Try telling the children to close their eyes and be led one after the other through a (safe) obstacle course only by having a hand on the shoulder of the person in front. Tell them they have been blinded by gas in the First World War. Ask them how they feel knowing they can never see their family again, or work to provide food for their children.

Ask the children to imagine they are on the Titanic and will be unable to board a lifeboat. Ask them to write a letter to their family for someone else to carry on to New York. There are hundreds of experiments to be done if you have time to prepare them. Reconstructive archaeology for example may be creating a Roundhouse out of twigs or lolly sticks to understand how it would fit together and the intelligence of the people who invented this technology. Try creating mud bricks as a class and discover how this would be done and which techniques from ancient peoples worked best.

Watching the Primitive Technology Youtube channel can give a fascinating insight to some experimental archaeology from the Stone Age.

https://www.youtube.com/channel/UCAL3JXZSzSm8AlZyD3nQdBA

Experimental archaeology does not necessarily mean you will reach the outcome you expect. Treat the experiment as you would any other and record the outcomes properly and discuss these with the children. Try building a shelter somewhere in the school grounds. Leave some different materials and tools that you deem safe for the age of children involved and allow them to build a shelter however they want but try to direct one group to build against a wall, others to build with shelter of trees and bushes, others to use the middle of the field or playground. Ask which were the easiest and hardest areas to build on.

Consider marking a river, or food sources such as hunting grounds or fruit bushes with cones or chalk. Ask which area they would prefer to sleep near and which materials they would prefer to transport long distances on their backs. Link this activity to the Stone Age and the migration of our ancestors. Why would they choose to build close to natural shelter or close to rivers or food sources? What if they had to choose between a food source or water source? What if they found other people living there already? It may also be possible to link this activity to orienteering to first collect the material to create a shelter and then extend further to create clues such as maths problems that must be solved before the orienteering co-ordinate is revealed though this may need to take place over a half or even full day.

'Tell me, and I'll listen,
Show me, and I'll understand,
Involve me, and I'll learn.'

—Lakota

http://www.leeds.ac.uk/educol/documents/00003003.htm
An article on the use of experimental archaeology in education.

https://exarc.net/keywords/children
Reports, articles and examples of experimental archaeology.

https://archaeology.mrdonn.org/
A website for both adults and children containing child friendly explanations on archeology and lesson plans and resources.

ICT

The use of ICT in history for children is a superb way to enable the research of their own interests. Biography work on famous people, places or events can be an excellent opportunity for children to research history and further their learning through the use of ICT. Beyond the creation of slideshows and resources, ICT can also be used in the role of learning through play such as the use of history games, video clips and information websites.

The use of ICT is often reduced to nothing more than ensuring children can code and use desktop computers properly, ignoring the fact that children can do more with their phones and tablets than most staff can do with theirs. The study of history requires some form of research and never has this been easier than in the age of the internet. Now, with home learning such a large part of school life, the use of ICT in the teaching and learning of history is more important than ever. There are a great many resources that are available online especially videos from experts and infographics shows.

The use of ICT for research can aid children with the skills of finding, categorising and selecting information which is relevant to their course of study. This skill of information literacy will be a valuable asset for children and will become an important part of their character, especially in today's world of fake news. Information literate children will find comprehension and reading tasks easier and will be able to select relevant information with comparative ease.

DT

There are an unlimited number of things you can create as individuals and groups for your topic. A Roman bulla purse is quick and easy to create. All you need is a circle of felt or leather and a piece of string. Cut a series of holes a few centimetres from the edge all the way around then thread the string through and pull to create a bulla purse. Oil lamps out of clay are also a favourite though these should always come with a fire risk warning. Create a cannon out of a cardboard box and rolled black paper, black painted corrugated cardboard or a wide mailing tube.

Making Roman Scutum shields out of cardboard and yoghurt pots or Viking shields from pizza box bases, yoghurt pots and quick dry plasters. Miniature viking shields added onto a viking ship tracing makes a fantastic display board. I have already mentioned food but this can also be done as part of DT. Roman mosaics of cut paper, Victorian printed wallpaper using sponges or styrofoam tiles is another great art/DT lesson especially if a few designs are sketched then different methods of printing are attempted. Afterwards review which worked best. Don't be afraid to go all out, consider blocking out a day or two for DT to get through a particular project.

Implement activities designed to get children working together to solve a problem as part of their DT work. If working on railways try building a spaghetti bridge capable of supporting a weight between two tables. The Romans built aqueducts to transport water, can the children in your class manage the same without instruction? Be creative and discuss ideas with colleagues.

Below I have given instructions for creating a shield.

To create a viking shield you will need:

- One pizza base cardboard or pizza box.
- One marker.
- Piece of string.
- Modroc.
- A round yoghurt pot.
- String.
- Glue.
- Aprons.
- Paint.

1. Draw a circle around the pizza base.
2. Punch two holes, the width of your hand apart +2cm in the centre of the shield.
3. Push string through the holes and create a small knot on the outside edge of the shield.
4. Attach with glue a yoghurt pot on the opposite side of the shield from the string to create a boss.
5. Cut the modroc into strips for half the size of your shield.
6. Dip the modroc into tepid water and squeeze the excess water out.
7. Place across the shield until completely covered.

8. Ensure modroc has secured the yoghurt pot and completely covers it.
9. Allow to dry.
10. Once dry paint as necessary. (Remember the shield boss should be metallic)

Once your shield has been created they become much more hardy than typical cardboard shields and can be used on displays or PE lessons.

Art

Art lessons can be wide ranging and varied when relating to history and many relate to them as their own topic in any case. Art is an expression of the soul in a way that words often fall short. A great deal of art records historical events, people and acts as a visual record to base further research and exploration from. The Bayeux Tapestry, Greek and Latin statues and Frescos are often preserved ways of life, showing us the morals, attitudes and expectations of both ancient and modern history.

Before the invention of the camera art was one of the few ways history could be recorded. Studying Norman Cornish for example offers a glimpse of the past of working towns and the people that lived there. Try to contact local art galleries or art museums in order to arrange a visit or ask for loan boxes, resources or activity ideas. Artwork can be an interesting foray into the way historical people lived. A good example of this is Stone Age art. Children can recreate cave paintings using charcoal and earthy chalk pastels, some study will need to be done beforehand as children often miss the method of replicating this artwork. Stone Age blow painting is another excellent example of historic art.

To do this you will need:

- 1 Piece of A4 paper. Preferable cartridge or similar.
- 1 Straw per child.
- Earthy colours of non-toxic, ready mixed poster paint.
- Aprons and table covers recommended.

1. First, cover the tables, roll up your sleeves, and put on an apron.
2. Place one hand in the centre of the paper with fingers spread wide.
3. Suck a little paint up into the straw. (NOT INTO YOUR MOUTH)
4. Blow the paint onto your hand and paper.
5. Repeat.
6. Do not remove your hand until satisfied with paint covering.
7. Allow to dry before displaying in your classroom cave.

https://www.bbc.co.uk/bitesize/topics/zsx6fg8/resources/1
These are a few videos on Art and it's place in history.

https://www.youtube.com/watch?v=ZjejoT1gFOc&ab_channel=NationalGeographic A video on cave art.

https://www.youtube.com/channel/UCR2NIUr0yPuqRxZN_7ItHog More videos on artists, not closely linked to history but well worth a look.

https://www.youtube.com/watch?v=iNPYnnCBhV0&ab_channel=CassieStephens A sketch prompt relating to Stone Henge

PE

For PE lessons try to incorporate your topic work at least once per term. Using the cannons you made you could do a gun run or disassemble the gun, move it piece by piece to another area then reassemble it. Try an assault course with the additional stipulation that it's part of the Western Front and you have to move back to your own lines across no mans land. Puzzle games such as the lifeboat exercise are also good ways of incorporating history into a PE lesson. Try historic sports such as javelin, running or marching together in a formation with the addition of the class made shields and foil wrapped cardboard swords.

Below I have included an activity that was done during a PE lesson, although not a particularly energetic activity it can be used as part of a carousel of other activities in small groups.

Lifeboat rescue

You will need:

- One large blanket, tablecloth or cover per group of 4-6 children.

You are a survivor of the Titanic but your lifeboat has flipped over! There are icebergs close by and you have to flip the lifeboat over. The only rule is you cannot step off the blanket at any time or you will be lost to the icy waters of the Atlantic. If you step off the lifeboat you can no longer help your team.

The children can now experiment as to how to turn the blanket over. Usually they try folding the blanket but quickly reach the conclusion that it won't work. The solution to this is for everyone to stand at one end, twist the blanket into an hourglass or farfalle shape then move to the other end and twist the other end so the entire blanket has been turned.

There are one or two other possible ways to succeed but it is best left to the children to discover. Modify existing PE activities to link to your history planning. Once an activity has been modified the first time the hard work is done and it can be reused. To link PE and history together there is a nearly unlimited possibility of activities with a little creativity and imagination. With a cupboard full of PE equipment ask children to build a structure linked to your history work, a castle for example. Let them decide how best to do this and make mistakes. See how quickly hoops become towers, ropes become drawbridges and moats.

Use your PE materials to create a team exercise such as a river crossing. The children must cross the river (marked by cones), they can't go in the water because there are crocodiles (small hurdles or large cones). They must cross the river because the Roman Army is chasing them so there is a time limit. The supplies they must carry across could be bean bags or balls. They must cross the river in inventive ways such as distracting the crocodiles with the supplies as they cross but then they have less to place in the bucket and the other team might win. Although only a tenuous link to history these sessions can create a more energetic interpretation of history and rather than teaching historical lessons it makes history more fun and engaging.

History in EYFS

When teaching history in EYFS learning through play will serve as a large part in most activities. Although history is not it's own section in the statutory requirement under the EYFS framework some links can be drawn between history and other statutory areas, though you should not feel that history should be a priority. Even during foundation stage children can be interested in their own history and will begin to learn the meaning of terms such as tomorrow, today and yesterday.

'Understanding the world - People and communities: children talk about past and present events in their own lives and in the lives of family members. They know that other children don't always enjoy the same things, and are sensitive to this. They know about similarities and differences between themselves and others, and among families, communities and traditions.' -EYFS Statutory framework.

The use of historical language, role play, dress up and work on world cultures can create good links with history and aid children being inquisitive and asking why things happen or are as they are. There are many suggested schemes of work for children in EYFS to follow but this is something which must be agreed upon by the EYFS team. Some resources and activities in this book may be useful to adapt and use in EYFS.

https://assets.publishing.service.gov.uk/government/uploads/system/uploads/attachment_data/file/596629/EYFS_STATUTORY_FRAMEWORK_2017.pdf This is a link to the EYFS statutory framework.

https://www.history.org.uk/primary/resource/9197/eyfs-scheme-of-work This is a link to an EYFS scheme of work centred on history.

History in Living Memory

Living memory is the part of history that people alive today can still remember. The Second World War will shortly pass from living memory and the experiences and memories that have not been recorded will be lost forever. People often consider history to be connected only to the large events. The lives of ordinary folk can often offer a more comprehensive understanding of the climate those events took place in.

History such as VE and VJ days, the end of the British Empire and partition of India, the end of rationing, the Cold War, Fall of the Berlin Wall and end of Apartheid are all in lving memory but never spring to mind when asked about the major historical events of the world. Consider for example the attacks on the World Trade Centre, commonly known as 9/11. This is now a part of worldwide living history and marks a change in the way the world thought and acted. Security measures sprung up almost overnight, a war on terror was declared and nothing has been the same since.

Covid 19 is something we are experiencing now, one day it may be talked about the same way as the Black Death, or maybe it will slide into obscurity before the end of the century. My point is that you should exploit the living memory of history whilst there is still the primary source in the eyewitness evidence of the people who lived through it. I expect that before long our own experiences will occupy some textbook or exam paper asking students to pick apart a source relating to the handling of CoronaVirus. I know that when I am asked about Covid-19 I will tell it all, the days when people decided doctors and scientists weren't worth listening to, but demanded children return to schools because their education was important so that they could be the next generation of doctors and scientists.

Home Learning/Busy Tray Activities

Below is a list of small scale, short term activities that can be used alongside the usual teaching of history to support immersion and children's own learning.

- Create a timeline of your favourite historical character.
- Write a story about your favourite historical character. Feel free to do research.
- Watch documentaries.
- Read books relating to the subject.
- Ensure the class reading area has books relating to the subject for free reading.
- Encourage children to perform show and tell relating to the history work.
- Write your name in hieroglyphs/Latin/Viking runes.
- Build your own stonehenge.
- Make a sundial from a paper plate and lolly stick.
- Build a castle from cardboard.
- Make a pomander.
- Create a family tree.
- Code a history game.
- Make an aqueduct that works.
- Learn Morse code.
- Make a stained glass window from cellophane.
- Dress up and role play history.

- Play history games.
- https://www.topmarks.co.uk/Search.aspx?Subject=13&AgeGroup=2 Interactive games.
- https://www.history.org.uk/primary/categories/resource-sharing-hub-primary A good resource for all kinds of history.
- Try craft work related to your topic.
- Create a portrait of a famous historical figure.
- Read historical poems or stories to your class.
- Ensure your reading area has age appropriate history books, both fiction and non-fiction.
- https://www.history.co.uk/ find more resources and ideas for your classroom here.
- Code your own history game.
- Historical figure egg jarping.
- Rainy Day resources for the classroom such as word searches, dot to dots and mazes related to the topic.

How History Links to Modern Issues

Part of understanding history is the ability to examine and validate sources of information. To be able to look at a piece of information and decide why it has been created and shared links closely to the modern day infodemic of fake news and sensationalist media. To have the critical skills of spotting biased, and misleading, one sided information and news is something that children must be equipped with to combat the information which is constantly available. Understanding how misinformation and manipulation has led to some of the worst events in world history can give us an understanding of why these things should not be tolerated and how they can be looked at critically.

By taking account of our past we can discover how we got to where we are now, and we can better choose our path for the future. Think about people you know who never learn from their mistakes, do they really understand the choices and circumstances that led them to where they are now? If they do, do they take responsibility or accept some of the blame? This is the same way we must view our current lives. The government we choose is decided by its past as much as it is by its future promises, we judge our students and employees by their past work, companies by their past reviews and products by our past experiences and yet when it comes to important decisions and events we seem to ignore the lessons history has taught us.

History shows us how to find the root and cause of problems and events and prioritise them then compare reactions to this and how the problem would have been best solved with the minimum disruption.

Below is an activity plan used in part of a Titanic topic at an extracurricular history club. It links with P4C and led to excellent discussions about morals, modern values and how small events can build up to larger ones. I have also included a lesson plan on studying sources of information and links to historical vocabulary. This lesson plan was intended for a year 5/6 class mix.

Lesson Plan

Teacher:

Context – Fact/opinion (Sources)

Learning Objective	Success Criteria
To explore a range of sources and examine their worth.	<ul><li>I can identify and explain the difference between fact and opinion.</li><li>I can decide if a source is untrustworthy and why.</li></ul>Children will be able to identify the differences between a fact and an opinion and articulate how they know the difference. Children will employ vocabulary such as 'bias(ed), trustworthy, primary, secondary, myth, legend, propaganda, rumour and fallacy' to select reputable sources.

Activity

Children in table groups will be provided with a range of sources and asked to order them from most trustworthy to least trustworthy. As a class we will then discuss their choices and ask for explanation as to why they think this. We will then examine these as a class and record our findings on an A3 sheet in groups. These will then be photocopied and stored in individual children's files.

Sources: Queen Elizabeth I Armada Portrait, Photograph of No Man's Land at The Somme, Diary entry of Samuel Pepys, textbook extract on Victorian schools, local parish record of marriages, modern artists reconstruction of a Roman Villa, excavated medieval village photograph.

Note: Previous lessons work on historical vocabulary should be present on desks for reference during this work.

History club planning

Lifeboat activity	
Resources needed Chairs for ⅔ of children involved Bibs to act as life vests Doll	Set up chairs into 3 groups, ensure that only six chairs are available per group of eight. Split children into groups of appx 8. Nominate one to be a deck officer in charge of selecting who goes into the lifeboats. Give the other children stickers. The stickers for two children should say sailor, the others can be 1st class male passenger, old lady, doctor, etc. The deck officers must allow their life boats to be filled though they will each be given different instructions. E.g. First class only, women and children first, women and children only. The 'passengers' must convince the deck officers they should be allowed on the lifeboat. Note stickers should not be awarded based on gender but completely random.
Objective: Children will learn how the lack of lifeboat seats, different interpretations of instructions and general confusion contributed to the loss of life on the Titanic.	**Key questions:** How did you choose who could and could not get onto a lifeboat? Did any officers choose to save themselves? Why? What did the passengers feel during their attempts to get onto the lifeboats? What would happen if a disaster like this happened today?

How could more people have been saved from the Titanic and what was the effect of it on maritime operations?

Conclusion

Discussing the ideas you have read in this book with other staff will lead to many adaptations of activities that will work better for your classroom than have worked in mine. Each person will think of activities slightly differently, don't worry if activities don't go as well as you'd hoped, adapt them or try different approaches. Typically the activities I have led have been held in classes of between 24 and 33 children though some were initially conceived for groups of 14.

You may have noticed I did not include sections on linking Numeracy or Literacy to the history topic, this is because the links for these are usually something covered by training courses and often arise in discussions as the typical planning for topics. These should still go ahead but I wanted to offer a much broader range of potential activities. Sometimes links are made for no other reason other than for the sake of making a link and this typically happens for Literacy. Almost every teacher will have at some point set their children the task of writing a diary entry as a historical figure and more often than not this lesson ends up being just another exercise of plan, polish, write and loses all value of being something vaguely connected to the history topic. By all means write a diary entry but focus on the content and the ideas rather than quibbling over where the Stone Age, prehistoric human writing the diary has placed a comma.

Some small things often crop up from the most unexpected places such as a parent commenting that they once had a themed teddy to sit with the table that produced the best work at the school they worked at which I then used myself and proved very successful, though mine only appeared during history work. Quickly nicknamed Henry the History Bear he became a classroom favourite. History is not considered one of the more important subjects in education which is a shame considering the historical degradation of education since the end of World War Two by aggressive budgeting, changes in curriculum and government meddling of targets to make themselves look good.

I maintain that history is an important factor in shaping young minds and ensuring that we don't forget the important lessons of history such as slavery, the Holocaust, imperialism, World Wars, possible nuclear annihalition and the utter disregard of the poor and destitute. World changing events should never be forgotten such as the Peasants Revolt, The Black Death, Fall of Rome, Battle of Trafalgar, End of the British Empire, Abolition of Slavery, Womens Suffrage, Legalisation of Gay Marriage and fall of the Berlin Wall. Some of these things are recorded now only by people who weren't there. Invite people who lived through eras you are studying when possible and listen to their stories and understand that soon everything they knew about that time will pass on into more pages of history books but some will be lost forever. It is these things that will be lost that we should seek to spark children's curiosity to seek out, understand and record these lost gems of the past before nothing remains at all.

After all, those who do not learn from history are doomed to repeat it. Or at least re-sit the exam.

Helpful Links

I have included some helpful links here which did not necessarily fit in the other sections of the book.

https://www.youtube.com/watch?v=YABES_D9xfE&ab_channel=RmxManOfficial
The first recorded sounds in history.

https://www.youtube.com/watch?v=fkxysRE3oug&ab_channel=VintageEveryday
The first film recorded fight.

https://www.youtube.com/watch?v=KnieUa2-22o&ab_channel=Lindybeige
A guide to the Bayeux Tapestry.

https://www.youtube.com/watch?v=hLE-5EIGIPM&ab_channel=TheSchoolofLife
An explanation of History.

https://www.southernswords.co.uk/
This is a useful link to buy historical weapons, clothing and armour.

http://www.historyinteractive.co.uk/nationalcurriculumkeystage2primaryhistory.html
A good link for multiple resources for multiple ages.

http://www.bbc.co.uk/history/interactive/games/
History games.

https://www.youtube.com/watch?v=1kZ-8wmDqqk&ab_channel=YEAP%21
How ancient languages sounded.

https://www.youtube.com/watch?v=8fxy6ZaMOq8&ab_channel=Yestervid
How the English language has changed.

https://www.history.org.uk/membership/info/primary
A paid subscription to a resource centre.

https://www.teachithistory.co.uk/
A good site for resources and planning.

http://www.primaryresources.co.uk/history/history.htm
A superb website for a range of resources.

https://don-benson.com/
The authors website. You can also find me on facebook under Don Benson Books!

Acknowledgments

I would like to thank the staff and children of every school for their constant contributions to the pages of this book, without dedicated staff and inquisitive children the teaching of history would stall forever. I am constantly amazed by the effort teachers put into their work and I wanted to write this book to grease the wheels a little when it comes to history. I would also like to thank my partner for their unwavering support and my constant badgering for them to check my books over for mistakes. If you find any, please blame them and not me. I would also like to thank E. R. Pickering for her hard work on designing the cover of this book, she is an excellent artist and I hope she will design many more covers for me in future.

For more of my books please visit
https://don-benson.com/books/ or check them out on the kindle store.

If you enjoyed my work consider supporting my future endeavours here.
https://www.patreon.com/DonBenson

Thank you for buying and reading my book!- Don.

The contents of this book and e-book are held under copyright to Don Benson. No part of this book may be copied, reproduced or otherwise used publicly without the express written consent of the author. All website links and their pages, and activities not created by the author are the property of their creators and appear only as suggestions. If you wish to copy, reproduce or distribute any part of this book contact the author via the website mentioned in the acknowledgements section.

Don Benson Books

Printed in Great Britain
by Amazon